T0197552

Copyright © 2015 by Pat Bryan. 671828

ISBN: Softcover   978-1-5035-2969-4
        Hardcover   978-1-5035-2971-7
        EBook   978-1-5035-2970-0

All rights reserved. No part of this book may be
reproduced or transmitted in any form or by any means,
electronic or mechanical, including photocopying, recording,
or by any information storage and retrieval system,
without permission in writing from the copyright owner.

Print information available on the last page.

Rev. date: 04/20/2015

To order additional copies of this book, contact:
Xlibris
1-888-795-4274
www.Xlibris.com
Orders@Xlibris.com

Shoes For Horses? was written in memory of:

My dad, Ken Baldwin, a horseshoer to remember

My mom, Eula, a feisty little lady

Bo, the best horse ever

Written for my children: Susan, Scott, and daughter-in-law Colleen

Dedicated to my granddaughter, Danielle, best known to me as Dani

Thanks to Colorado farrier Wes McAndrew for his pink one liner, and to Bill Faulkner who continues horseshoeing in the tradition of my dad. Thanks to my friends Kathy Baker, Kathleen Tresemer, Mary Lamphere and the Xlibris staff for helping this book happen.

Dani and Bo

Shoes For Horses?

Grandma was just finishing washing breakfast dishes when she heard a familiar sound, giggles!

Grandchildren Susan and Scottie were returning from the barn. Grandpa was not very far behind. They had been feeding Bo, the horse.

"Have you two been eating feather soup?" asked Grandma.

"Oh, Grandma. There's no such thing as feather soup."

"Well, something is tickling you," Grandma replied.

Through giggles, Susan said, "Grandpa said that Bo is getting new shoes today. Horses don't wear shoes."

"Oh, but they do," Grandpa replied. "Just not the kind you're thinking of."

Grandma started to giggle as she imagined horses wearing people shoes.

She pictured a circus horse wearing clown shoes.

She was certain a work horse would wear work boots just like Grandpa's.

What kind of shoes would a spotted Indian pony wear? Moccasins!

Oh, and a horse lying down –
loafing, perhaps – that horse would be wearing loafers.

8

A race horse would be wearing the fastest tennis shoes available.

9

Fancy Arabian horses should have high heels.

What would a quarter horse like Bo wear? Sometimes he wore a saddle, so Grandma laughed out loud as she imagined him wearing – what else? Saddle shoes.

The neighbors raised miniature horses. Grandma thought they would wear Mary Janes. What a sight.

As Grandma imagined shoes for horses, Grandpa noticed the horse shoer was driving his truck to the barn. "Come on kids. Kids, this is Ken," Grandpa said. "Ken, I'd like you to meet our grandkids, Susan and Scottie. This is the first time they've heard about horses wearing shoes. Ken was glad to meet the kids, and he asked, "Would you like to see some shoes?" "Sure," the children said.

"Here they are."

"Wow," remarked Scottie, "That's just like what Grandpa has hanging above the barn door."

"You're right. And notice the shoe is hung with the open end up. The shoe is hung up there for good luck. If you hang it upside down, the luck will run out."

The kids were learning a lot that day.

Susan, dressed in pink from head to toe, asked, "Do you have any pink shoes?"

Grandpa just knew that Bo was thinking, *"Pink? Oh, I hope not!"* Ken told Susan that the shoes only came in black.

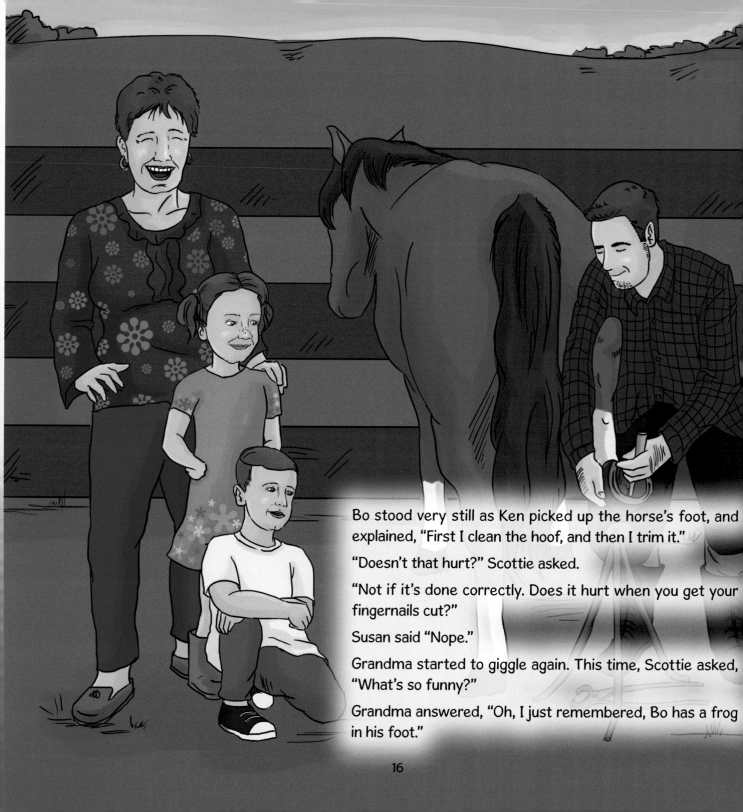

Bo stood very still as Ken picked up the horse's foot, and explained, "First I clean the hoof, and then I trim it."

"Doesn't that hurt?" Scottie asked.

"Not if it's done correctly. Does it hurt when you get your fingernails cut?"

Susan said "Nope."

Grandma started to giggle again. This time, Scottie asked, "What's so funny?"

Grandma answered, "Oh, I just remembered, Bo has a frog in his foot."

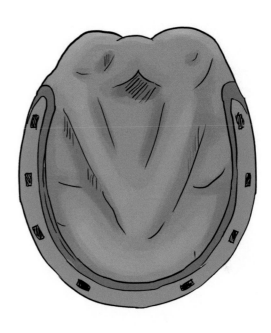

"What?" The kids were waiting for a little green frog to jump out.

Ken said, "Don't let her fool you. There is a frog, but not the kind you're thinking of. Look here." Ken showed them that a frog is the triangle-shaped part of the bottom of a horse's foot that acts as a cushion when the foot hits the ground. "See?"

"Doesn't look like a frog to me," Scottie said, disappointed.

"Scottie, would you hand me that shoe, please? Let's see if it fits."

Ken lifted Bo's foot, tried on the shoe, and said, "It fits. Let's nail it on."

"Nail it on?" both kids asked.

Susan exclaimed, "Oh, my gosh! I can't watch."

18

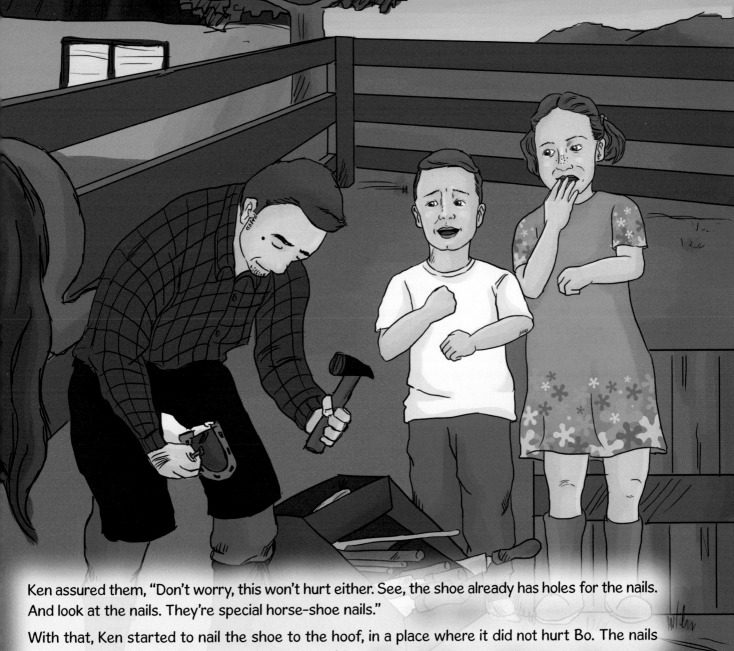

Ken assured them, "Don't worry, this won't hurt either. See, the shoe already has holes for the nails. And look at the nails. They're special horse-shoe nails."

With that, Ken started to nail the shoe to the hoof, in a place where it did not hurt Bo. The nails went into the bottom of the hoof, and out the side.

When all eight nails were in place, Ken took a big clipper and clipped off the ends of the nails. Then he took a rasp and smoothed the ends of the nails, so the rough edges wouldn't stick out. He did the same to all four feet and, and then drove away to the next horses waiting for attention.

That night, when the kids were asleep, Grandma and Grandpa recalled the events of the day.

"I'm glad the kids were here when Ken came. They learned a lot today, and had fun too," said Grandpa.

With a big smile on his face, Grandpa said, "I forgot to tell the kids that some horses have socks; some have stockings."

Grandma had to laugh, as she realized the kids would imagine people socks. "Grandpa, I think that's another story."

20

Printed in the United States
By Bookmasters